TABLE OF
CONTENTS

IRAs & Annuities

How to Strengthen Your Financial Base As You Move Toward Retirement

MOODY PRESS
CHICAGO

All Scripture quotations, unless indicated, are taken from the *Holy Bible: New International Version*. Copyright © 1973, 1978, 1984, International Bible Society. Used by permission of Zondervan Publishing House. All rights reserved.

ISBN 0-8024-3993-4

Library of Congress Cataloging in Publication Data

1 3 5 7 9 10 8 6 4 2

Printed in the United States of America

FOREWORD

I have known Austin Pryor for almost twenty years now, and I regard him as a good friend. As I have observed him over the years, I have found his counsel to be both biblical and practical. I know of no other individual with whom I would consult with more confidence on the subject of mutual fund investing than Austin.

I believe the true character of an investment adviser is not only the degree of success he has achieved, but the integrity that is maintained in the process. Austin has achieved success in the business world, but, more important, he has done so with truth and honesty.

Obviously you, the reader, must evaluate his advice yourself. No one individual has the right advice for everyone, and anyone can, and will, be wrong in the changing economy we live in. But if you will spend the time to read carefully the counsel Austin provides, you will find it both time and money well spent.

I encouraged my good friends at Moody Press to contact Austin about publishing his writing because I felt he had information that would benefit God's people. We are in no way competitors. Austin and I are collaborators in God's plan to help His people become better stewards of His resources.

Larry Burkett

The biblical principles reflected in this booklet are the foundation for the advice given in *Sound Mind Investing*, my book published by Moody Press. The material in this booklet has, for the most part, been excerpted from that book. As Christians, we acknowledge God as the owner of all. We serve as His stewards with management privileges and responsibilities. The practical application of biblical principles leads us to encourage a debt-free lifestyle and conservative approach to investing such as that shown in what we call the Four Levels of Investing:

Level One: Getting Debt-Free
"The rich rules over the poor, and the borrower becomes the lender's slave."
Proverbs 22:7

Paying off debts which are carrying 12%-18% per year interest charges is the best "investment" move you can make. So, get to work on paying off those credit cards, car loans, student loans, and other short-term debts. Accelerating the payments on your house mortgage, if any, should also be your goal—albeit a longer-term one. It should be your first priority to see the day when you're meeting all current living expenses, supporting the Lord's causes, and completely free of consumer debt.

Level Two: Saving for Future Needs
"There is precious treasure and oil in the dwelling of the wise, but a foolish man swallows it up." Proverbs 21:20

Even if you've not completely reached your Level One goal, it's still a good idea to set aside some money for emergencies or large purchases. A prudent rule of thumb is that your contingency fund should be equal to three to six months' living expenses. We suggest $10,000 as an amount suitable for most family situations.

Level Three: Investing in Stocks

*"Well done, good and faithful servant. You were faithful with a few things,
I will put you in charge of many things." Matthew 25:21*

Only money you have saved over and above the funds set aside in
Level Two should be considered for investing in the stock market.
In Levels One and Two, any monthly surplus was used in a manner
that *guaranteed* you would advance financially—there are no guar-
antees in the stock market. You should initiate a program of stock
mutual fund investing geared to your personal risk temperament
and the amount of dollars you have available to invest.

Level Four: Diversifying for Safety

*"Divide your portion to seven, or even to eight, for you do not know what
misfortune may occur on the earth." Ecclesiastes 11:2*

Once you accumulate $25,000 in your investment account, it's time
for further diversification. By adding investments to your holdings
that "march to different drummers," you can create a more efficient,
less volatile portfolio. The single most important diversification
decision is deciding how much to invest in stocks versus bonds.
That's why determining your personal investing temperament, and
following the guidelines given, can be so helpful.

Free Upon Request

Articles that guide you through the Four Levels—help on getting
debt-free, saving strategies, and updates on specific no-load mutual
fund recommendations that are geared to your personal risk tolerance—appear in my monthly newsletter, also called *Sound Mind
Investing*. In it, I offer a conservative investing strategy based on the
careful use of no-load mutual funds. For a free sample copy, simply
return the postage-paid card included at the back of this booklet.

How Much Will It Cost to Live in Prime Time?

I. As the baby-boomer generation moves into retirement, the 65-and-over age group will grow from 12% at present to 20% of the total population. The need for adequate retirement planning will grow too.

A. Today's retirees are the wealthiest in U.S. history. With life expectancies of about 15 years following retirement, the vast majority of them live out their lives quite comfortably.

B. As life expectancies continue to increase, the baby-boomer generation can reasonably expect to live 20-25 years past retirement.

C. Longer life expectancies and the increasing cost of health care indicate that today's workers must plan carefully to be sure of financial security during retirement.

II. Projecting your income needs at retirement involves a two-step process.

A. You must project your post-retirement budget by making adjustments in your current budget to reflect the changes that accompany retirement.

B. You must allow for the effects of inflation.

C. Your projected income needs at retirement may appear daunting. We should be comforted by God's promise to meet all our needs "according to his glorious riches in Christ Jesus."

When I was a small child, perhaps eight or so, it used to fascinate me to think that someday I'd be "old" like my parents.

My mother was 21 when I was born, and I used to say to her (proud of my newly acquired ability to add numbers), "Mom! When I'm 21, you'll be 42!" And she'd answer back, "And when you're 42, I'll be 63!" Knowing it was my turn to go next, I would usually begin giggling at what to me was a really silly idea; namely, that I would *ever* be 63 or that she would *ever* be 84!

I could imagine being old enough to go to high school someday, and maybe college after that. I could almost imagine being old enough to get married, although I wasn't at all sure why I would ever want to. But picturing myself as being over 60, like my grandparents, was simply incomprehensible, beyond the limits of my youthful imagination. So I laughed because it seemed so silly.

I recalled my little childhood game recently as I read some fascinating statistics on what's been called "the graying of America." Did you know that today's generation of retirees (I'll call them "prime-timers") are the wealthiest in U.S. history? They participated in the postwar economic boom, watched their homes greatly escalate in value during the inflationary 1970s, and paid far less into pension plans and Social Security than they are now taking out in indexed benefits. At the same time, the children are grown and out on their own, most mortgages are paid off, and work-related expenses are no longer a drag on the family budget.

The vast majority of Americans 65 and older are living comfortably. Taken as a whole...

...they have an average net worth of around $100,000 per household. According to a report based on 1990 census data published in *American Demographics* magazine, 75% own their own homes, almost 80% have savings that average $20,000, and more than 20% have another $11,000 in stock and bond portfolios.

The number of those joining the ranks of the retired is increasing at twice the rate of the overall population. By the year 2030, the post WWII "baby boomers" will raise the prime-timer population to 64 million. This translates to about one out of every five Americans, up from only one in every eight now. What will retirement be like for us newcomers? (Although I was born a year too early to officially be a boomer, I'm taking a little editorial license and including myself anyway.) Will we have it as good? The trends are not encouraging.

Somewhat paradoxically, the problem has to do with the fact that life expectancy continues to make remarkable gains. This increasing longevity is due mainly to the continuing improvements in health care; also contributing to longer lives is the American public's discovery of the benefits of nutrition, physical fitness, and healthier lifestyles. About 80% of prime-timers consider their health excellent, good, or fair. A significant decline in activities and interests doesn't generally occur until age 85 and later.

It now seems that moving into the 85+ group has the "elderly" connotation formerly associated with the 65+ group. One expert refers to them as "old-olds..."

...to distinguish them from the "young-olds" who are *only* 65 to 84. The old-olds population is growing fast, projected to exceed 8 million by 2030. The odds of living to age 100 are now down to just 87-1. The number of centenarians will triple   in the next 10 years; more than 35,000 are now at least age 100.

In short, we'll all be living longer. And let's face it: living costs money.

Of course, the longer the life, the greater likelihood that support services will be needed; families now stand a greater chance than ever before of having a disabled elderly relative to support. More than 80% of us will enjoy reasonably good health, but even so, it's estimated that health care for prime-timers costs three to four times what it costs the rest of the population.

Then there are the other niceties of everyday life, such as food, shelter, clothing, and recreation. And whereas the current generation of retirees could reasonably expect to live (and budget for) only about 15 years as prime-timers, boomers should probably add another 5-10 years to that. The current I.R.S. life expectancy tables indicate that a married couple entering retirement at age 65 should plan on one of them living to age 90.

First, we need to consider how our income needs will change as we enter retirement. The good news is that we can expect to maintain approximately our same standard of living in spite of our lower incomes. Here's why:

- We won't have work-related expenses such as commuting, eating away from home, and wardrobe maintenance.

- We won't have the children to feed, clothe, transport, and educate.

- We won't have the burden of paying Social Security and other payroll taxes.

- We won't be contributing to our personal and employer's retirement plans.

- And assuming we arrive at retirement debt-free, we won't have home mortgage payments, car payments, or credit card payments to make.

Of course, as I've already pointed out, we'll be facing increased health care costs, and since we'll have more free time, greater recreational expenditures. But all in all, most experts say that if your retirement income is around 75% of what you're earning now, you'll be in good shape; however, you're likely to face financial difficulties if it drops below 50% of what you're now making.

Let's see how this works. I'm going to pick a family out of the mid-range of the census data and assume we are preparing a projection for them. Let's call them the Millers. They are 35 years old and have current income (before taxes) of $40,000 per year. What will their annual income needs be when they retire?

To be on the conservative side, I'm going to use the 80% assumption. By multiplying that figure times their current income, we learn that the Millers will want to budget $32,000 per year income for their prime-time years. But that assumes their $32,000 will always buy for them what it can buy today, and we know that's not going to be the case.

We have to allow for the effects of inflation. The consumer price index provides some guidance, although your family's spending pattern is unique. Your personal inflation experience will be different from any theoretical number computed for the "typical" American family. After considering a number of arguments on the matter, I've decided to assume a 6% annual inflation rate for our planning purposes. It's a higher number than the official rate has been running, but not to the extreme levels of the critics.

Our next step, then, is to take the $32,000 per year we projected as the Millers' annual income need during retirement...

...and translate that to a higher number to allow for the fact that the value of the dollar shrinks a little every year. To do that, we refer to the inflation chart on this page. Since the Millers have 30 years to go before they reach age 65, we look down the left-hand column until we come to the number 30. And, since I've assumed long-term inflation will average 6% per year, we go over one column to find the number listed under the 6% heading.

(Note: I've included higher inflation numbers for your convenience if you want to raise the inflation assumption. Choosing the 8% rate,

INFLATION CHART

Years Until Retirement	Rates of Inflation		
	6%	8%	10%
5	1.34	1.47	1.61
6	1.42	1.59	1.77
7	1.50	1.71	1.95
8	1.59	1.85	2.14
9	1.69	2.00	2.36
10	1.79	2.16	2.59
11	1.90	2.33	2.85
12	2.01	2.52	3.14
13	2.13	2.72	3.45
14	2.26	2.94	3.80
15	2.40	3.17	4.18
16	2.54	3.43	4.59
17	2.69	3.70	5.05
18	2.85	4.00	5.56
19	3.03	4.32	6.12
20	3.21	4.66	6.73
21	3.40	5.03	7.40
22	3.60	5.44	8.14
23	3.82	5.87	8.95
24	4.05	6.34	9.85
25	4.29	6.85	10.83
26	4.55	7.40	11.92
27	4.82	7.99	13.11
28	5.11	8.63	14.42
29	5.42	9.32	15.86
30	5.74	10.06	17.45
31	6.09	10.87	19.19
32	6.45	11.74	21.11
33	6.84	12.68	23.23
34	7.25	13.69	25.55
35	7.69	14.79	28.10
36	8.15	15.97	30.91
37	8.64	17.25	34.00
38	9.15	18.63	37.40
39	9.70	20.12	41.14
40	10.29	21.72	45.26

for example, is for the extra cautious person who wants to be doubly careful to arrive at retirement with a sufficient nest egg built up.)

The number we find is 5.74. Now, here comes the scary part. We multiply $32,000 times 5.74 to learn what the Millers' income will need to be when they retire in 2021 in order to maintain their current standard of living. The answer is a whopping $183,680 per year! Sort of overwhelming, isn't it? It's difficult to imagine that the day will come when a family would need that much money *every year* just to maintain a modest lifestyle.

But don't despair. Inflation can be harnessed to work for you...

...as well as against you. Before this booklet is completed, you'll have been given enough information to enable you to overcome three of the four most common elements of financial failure:

❶ **A failure to inquire.** Many are ignorant of the serious financial implications of our changing society and how they will be affected.

❷ **A failure to learn.** Once made aware, they may still lack the know-how needed to begin putting their financial house in order.

❸ **A failure to plan.** Even informed, knowledgeable people can let years go by without formulating goals and a strategy for achieving them.

But after I inform you of the seriousness of the situation, teach you the basics of survival, and lead you through the planning process, there's still one element that only you can overcome:

❹ **A failure to act.** Procrastination can be the greatest deterrent to reaching your financial goals. If you're like I was as a child, acting as if you'll never grow old, you've been losing valuable time. Commit yourself now to making the sacrifices needed to put your family's finances on a solid foundation.

As you contemplate the challenges ahead, meditate on the promises of God given to us in Philippians 4:

Do not be anxious about anything, but in everything, by prayer and petition, with thanksgiving, present your requests to God. And the peace of God, which transcends all understanding, will guard your hearts and your minds in Christ Jesus...I have learned to be content whatever the circumstances. I know what it is to be in need, and I know what it is to have plenty. I have learned the secret of being content in any and every situation, whether well fed or hungry, whether living in plenty or in want. I can do everything through him who gives me strength...And my God will meet all your needs according to his glorious riches in Christ Jesus (verses 6-7, 11-13, and 19). ◆

Your Personal Pension: The Ins and Outs of IRAs

I. **The Individual Retirement Account can play a key role in your retirement investing strategy. Its appeal is twofold.**

   A. You might qualify for a tax deduction for your IRA contribution, up to a maximum of $2,000 a year.

   B. All the earnings in your IRA compound tax-deferred until you begin taking them out at retirement.

II. **The control you have over your IRA makes it very flexible.**

   A. You select the financial organization with whom you do business.

   B. You control how its assets are invested.

   C. You decide whether to contribute each year, and if so, how much.

   D. You select the timing and amount of your withdrawals.

III. To assist you with your long-range planning, two compound interest tables are presented, which show expected returns at various rates of interest over the next 1 to 50 years.

A. The "Compounded Growth of $1,000" table can be used to project the future value of an amount of money you currently have available for investing.

B. The "Compounded Growth of a $25 Monthly Contribution" table can be used to project the value of a series of monthly investments you will make in the future.

Your retirement income rests on what has been referred to as a three-legged stool. Social Security has traditionally been regarded as the first...

...of the three legs; however, the problems with Social Security make it impossible to project with confidence the level of monthly benefits 20 years and more into the future. Historically, the program has provided 35%-45% of retirees' monthly income; to be on the conservative side, you can use a lower assumption to reflect the uncertainty. Private employer-sponsored pension plans are the second leg, and provide about 15%-20% of retirees monthly income *on average* according to the Social Security Administration. But there's a lot of room for variation here. For workers who spend most of their careers with the same company, it would not be unusual for them to receive a pension equal to 30%-40% of what they were making at the time of retirement. In any event, it is obvious that the third leg of personal savings and retirement funds will continue to play a very important role in providing adequate retirement incomes.

One of the best ways to go about building your personal retirement funds is by using the tax-deferred Individual Retirement Account (IRA).

The IRA first appeared on the financial scene in 1981 when Congress voted to allow working persons to put away up to $2,000 a year for retirement *and deduct it* from their federal income tax return. Not only did they enjoy immediate tax savings, but they also were excused from paying any income taxes on the investment profits they made. Until they began withdrawing the money upon retirement, they had the pleasure of watching their money grow tax-deferred. After the deductibility of home mortgage interest, it was the best tax break available to the middle class.

Congress soon decided it had been too generous in allowing middle class taxpayers to keep so much of their own income. In passing the 1986 Tax Reform Act, our elected leaders decided to modify the rules. Congress limited the deductibility of IRA contributions to those folks who were not participating in retirement plans at work *unless their income fell below certain levels*. Although the 1986 tax law changes made IRAs less attractive for some, it's been estimated that 75% of IRA owners were unaffected by the changes.

Despite the modifications, the Individual Retirement Account should remain a key building block for almost everyone's retirement planning. The appeal is twofold.

First, you might still be able to take a tax deduction for all or part of your annual contribution. *If neither you nor your spouse is covered by a pension plan at work, your IRA contributions remain fully tax deductible.* The maximum amount you can contribute is equal to the lesser of (1) $2,000, or (2) your total compensation. For couples with one working spouse, the limit is $2,250. However, if both spouses work, the maximum contribution is raised to $4,000. This opportunity is available to everyone under age 70½ who earns income from employment (including self-employment). Even if you are covered at work, you can still make a contribution. A sliding scale, based on income, comes into play to determine how much of your contribution is deductible.

But the tax deduction is just one of the benefits. All the earnings inside an IRA compound tax-deferred until April 15 of the year after you reach age 70½. This is such a great benefit that, assuming you're debt free and can afford it, you should consider making an IRA contribution even if it is not all tax deductible. Earnings on nondeductible contributions, just like the earnings on fully deductible contributions, are not subject to Federal income tax until such time as they are withdrawn.

An IRA is not, in and of itself, an investment. It's merely a tax-shelter...

...that you put your investments *in*. IRAs can contain a wide variety of investments of your choosing. To get the most from the tax-deferred advantage, put your higher risk/reward type investments in it (as you're allocating risk according to one of the four temperaments) that you believe have the greater growth potential. Don't invest in tax-exempt securities like municipal bonds and annuities *in your IRA*. There's no point in putting investments that are already tax-exempt into an IRA; there's no additional tax savings. With municipal bonds, you're lowering your investment potential as well as, ironically, turning the interest from them (which would ordinarily be tax-free) into income that is taxable. Why? Because all your earnings are taxed when you withdraw them, even the earnings that come from otherwise tax-exempt investments.

Moving your IRA to a new trustee/custodian is a very simple matter. If you would like greater investment flexibility...

...the IRS allows you to transfer the assets in your IRA to a new custodian (I recommend either a no-load fund organization or the Charles Schwab Company) without paying any taxes or upsetting your tax-deferred status. The best way is to have your new custodian do it for you. Once you sign the authorization forms they provide, they will take care of the paperwork in what is called a trustee-to-trustee transfer. It couldn't be easier! The only stipulation is that you have to allow 12 months to pass before you are allowed to transfer the same IRA again.

If you have more than one IRA account, you might consider combining them into one.

It's not unusual for people to have many different IRAs spread around various places that were offering the "best deal" at the time their contribution was made. By combining them into one account at a no-load mutual fund organization, you'll save on annual account fees and cut your paper work. More important, you'll have a much easier time managing your investments and tracking their performance.

It's worth moving your IRA where it can get better returns even if they amount to only 2%-3% a year. For example, someone with $10,000 in his IRA who earns 8% a year will have $68,485 in 25 years. But if he could earn 10% instead, he'd have $108,347. That extra $40,000 provides additional years of monthly income once he retires.

Generally, you can begin taking money out of your IRA without penalty...

...once you reach age 59½. The longer you wait, the longer your money grows tax-deferred. The latest you can wait to begin making withdrawals is April 1 of the year *after* you reach age 70½.

The general rule is that your withdrawals are taxed as ordinary income in the year you receive them. Things get slightly more complicated if you've made nondeductible contributions because they've already been taxed. In that case, part of your withdrawal is taxed and part of it is treated simply as a return of your nondeductible contribution.

If you withdraw before reaching age 59½, you are vulnerable to a 10% penalty that is in addition to any tax you owe.

The 10% penalty is applied to the taxable amount of your withdrawal. The penalty does not apply if you have a disability, or if you begin a series of scheduled annuity payments based on your life expectancy. Any amount in your IRA at the time of your death is distributed to your named beneficiaries.

Remember that when you begin withdrawing funds during retirement, you'll pay taxes at that time. *Being tax-deferred is not the same as being tax-free.* Anyone willing to settle for the lower money market returns would likely be better off with municipal bonds (rather than adding to an IRA) because they are truly tax-free.

How much should you strive to have in your IRA upon retirement? How much is enough?

Let's return to the Millers (from Section One). They represented a typical American couple, based on the 1990 census data, whom we were helping with their retirement planning. When last we saw them, we had projected their income needs when they retire in 2022 to be $183,680 per year (assuming an average 6% rate of inflation). Picking from the historical rules of thumb suggested by the Social Security Adminstration, I'll assume that the Millers will receive 60% of their retirement income needs from their Social Security and employer-sponsored pensions. This amounts to $110,208 per year, leaving $73,472 to be provided by their own personal savings and retirement accounts. Remember, this is the amount of *income* they need, not the amount of capital.

To translate this into how much capital they should have accumulated, we simply divide it by the rate of return assumption. If they assume they can earn, on average, 9% per year on their investments, here's how to calculate the capital needed: $73,472 divided by .09 = $816,356. Now let's see how close the Millers will come to this amount.

First, let's assume that the Millers have been depositing into their IRAs for the past few years and now have total assets of $12,300. What will that grow to over the coming 30 years? Using the table at left, we see that $1,000 will grow to $13,268 in 30 years at an average return of 9%. Since the Millers have $12,300, we need to multiply the number in the table by 12.3. This gives a total projected IRA account value of $163,196 in 2022 even if they never deposited another dollar.

But they *do* plan to continue putting money into their IRA. From their monthly budget, they believe they can contribute $125 monthly throughout the year. That would total $1,500 annually, still below the $2,000 maximum allowable to them. Using the table at right, we see that a $25 monthly contribution will grow to $46,112 at 9% over 30 years. Since the Millers are putting aside $125 monthly—5 times that amount—we multiply $46,112 times 5 and arrive at a projected value for their future monthly contributions of $230,560. We can add this to the $163,196 projected growth target of their present holdings and arrive at a total projected IRA valuation of

THE COMPOUNDED GROWTH OF $1,000 INVESTMENT OVER TIME

You can use this table to see what your portfolio will be worth in the future, depending on the rate of return you receive. Miller example: They have $12,300 today and assume they will earn 9% over the next 30 years. What will it be worth then? Answer: $13,268 x 12.3 = $163,196.

After Year	5% Return	6% Return	7% Return	8% Return	9% Return	10% Return
6	1340	1419	1501	1587	1677	1772
7	1407	1504	1606	1714	1828	1949
8	1477	1594	1718	1851	1993	2144
9	1551	1689	1838	1999	2172	2358
10	1629	1791	1967	2159	2367	2594
11	1710	1898	2105	2332	2580	2853
12	1796	2012	2252	2518	2813	3138
13	1886	2133	2410	2720	3066	3452
14	1980	2261	2579	2937	3342	3797
15	2079	2397	2759	3172	3642	4177
16	2183	2540	2952	3426	3970	4595
17	2292	2693	3159	3700	4328	5054
18	2407	2854	3380	3996	4717	5560
19	2527	3026	3617	4316	5142	6116
20	2653	3207	3870	4661	5604	6727
21	2786	3400	4141	5034	6109	7400
22	2925	3604	4430	5437	6659	8140
23	3072	3820	4741	5871	7258	8954
24	3225	4049	5072	6341	7911	9850
25	3386	4292	5427	6848	8623	10835
26	3556	4549	5807	7396	9399	11918
27	3733	4822	6214	7988	10245	13110
28	3920	5112	6649	8627	11167	14421
29	4116	5418	7114	9317	12172	15863
30	4322	5743	7612	10063	13268	17449
31	4538	6088	8145	10868	14462	19194
32	4765	6453	8715	11737	15763	21114
33	5003	6841	9325	12676	17182	23225
34	5253	7251	9978	13690	18728	25548
35	5516	7686	10677	14785	20414	28102
36	5792	8147	11424	15968	22251	30913
37	6081	8636	12224	17246	24254	34004
38	6385	9154	13079	18625	26437	37404
39	6705	9704	13995	20115	28816	41145
40	7040	10286	14974	21725	31409	45259
41	7392	10903	16023	23462	34236	49785
42	7762	11557	17144	25339	37318	54764
43	8150	12250	18344	27367	40676	60240
44	8557	12985	19628	29556	44337	66264
45	8985	13765	21002	31920	48327	72890

$393,756. As large as this amount sounds, we are still $422,600 below the target of $816,356. Now what happens?

The Millers go back to the drawing board, tighten their belts, and come up with another $40 a month from their budget that they can add to their IRA. This raises the monthly contribution to $165 (for a total of $1,980 yearly), and increases the projected value of their future contributions to $304,339 ($46,112 times 6.6). The extra $40 a month translates into an extra $73,779 when you look 30 years down the road. This cuts the projected shortfall to $348,821, and seems to be all they can do for now.

Looking 12 years ahead, however, they realize they will finish paying off their home mortgage. When that time arrives, they had planned on taking their $843 a month payment and putting half into savings and the other half into "making life a little easier" as far as meeting the monthly budget was concerned. How could that money best be used to help make up their projected retirement shortfall? Since they're already right at the $2,000 maximum IRA contribution, they can't put anymore there. What else could they do that, while it might not be tax-deductible, still enjoys the advantage of tax-deferred compounding? Here is where annuities can play a key role in retirement planning. ◆

THE COMPOUNDED GROWTH OF A $25 MONTHLY IRA CONTRIBUTION

How quickly will a tax-deferred account grow if you make regular monthly deposits? Miller example: If they deposit $125 monthly, and assume a 9% rate of return over the next 30 years, what will it be worth then? Answer: $46,112 x 5 (Because $125 is 5 times $25) = $230,560.

After Year	5% Return	6% Return	7% Return	8% Return	9% Return	10% Return
6	2103	2171	2242	2316	2393	2471
7	2519	2615	2716	2822	2933	3046
8	2956	3086	3224	3369	3523	3682
9	3415	3586	3768	3962	4168	4384
10	3898	4117	4352	4604	4874	5160
11	4406	4681	4979	5300	5646	6016
12	4940	5280	5650	6053	6491	6963
13	5501	5916	6370	6868	7415	8008
14	6090	6590	7142	7752	8426	9163
15	6710	7307	7970	8709	9531	10439
16	7362	8067	8858	9745	10740	11849
17	8047	8875	9810	10867	12063	13406
18	8766	9732	10831	12082	13509	15127
19	9523	10642	11925	13398	15092	17027
20	10319	11609	13099	14824	16822	19127
21	11155	12635	14358	16367	18715	21446
22	12034	13724	15707	18039	20786	24008
23	12958	14880	17154	19850	23051	26839
24	13929	16108	18706	21811	25528	29965
25	14950	17411	20370	23934	28238	33420
26	16023	18795	22154	26234	31202	37236
27	17151	20264	24067	28725	34444	41451
28	18337	21824	26119	31422	37990	46108
29	19583	23480	28318	34344	41869	51253
30	20893	25238	30677	37507	46112	56936
31	22270	27105	33206	40934	50752	63214
32	23718	29087	35919	44645	55828	70150
33	25240	31191	38827	48663	61381	77813
34	26839	33424	41945	53016	67454	86277
35	28521	35796	45289	57729	74096	95628
36	30288	38314	48875	62834	81362	105958
37	32146	40987	52719	68363	89309	117369
38	34099	43825	56842	74350	98002	129976
39	36152	46837	61263	80834	107510	143903
40	38309	50036	66003	87857	117911	159288
41	40578	53432	71086	95462	129287	176284
42	42962	57038	76537	103699	141730	195059
43	45468	60866	82381	112619	155340	215801
44	48103	64930	88648	122280	170227	238715
45	50872	69244	95368	132743	186510	264028

SUMMARY

1. An IRA is a personal retirement fund for employed persons.

2. The money you put in is called a "contribution" and gets to grow tax-deferred until you take it out at retirement.

3. Once you're debt-free, you should definitely have one.

4. You can open one at most banks, brokers, mutual funds, and insurance companies. If they manage the investments, they're called the "trustee."

6. A "self-directed" IRA lets you manage the investments yourself, in which case the financial institution merely holds them for you as "custodian."

7. You can open an IRA at one place and easily move it to another.

8. If you take possession of your IRA money while moving your account, the IRS will have 20% of your account withheld for taxes. It's better to stay out of the picture and let your old IRA trustee pass your money directly to your new IRA trustee. Charles Schwab, as well as most mutual fund organizations, will handle asset transfers if you want to move your IRA to them.

9. You qualify to have an IRA no matter how high your earned income.

10. You may be able to take a tax deduction for your

contribution, depending on whether you are also participating in a retirement plan where you work and your level of income. In the long run, the advantage of tax-deferred growth is much more important than whether your contribution is deductible.

11. Make your IRA contributions early each year (January, if possible) so the money can begin growing tax-deferred. Depositing a little each month is also good. Waiting until the April 15 deadline wastes 15½ months.

12. You can take the money out at age 55 without penalty if you've taken early retirement. Otherwise, you can start at age 59½.

13. If need be, you can take money out of your IRA before retirement. You'll have to pay some income taxes, and there's a 10% penalty. You can avoid the penalty if you set up a schedule of "substantially equal" periodic payments.

14. You can borrow from your IRA under certain approved conditions. Check with your trustee/custodian for the specifics.

15. In the long run, the advantages of tax-deferred compounding outweigh the disadvantage of the taxes and potential penalty.

16. IRAs make nice presents for your children if they have W-2 or 1099 income. You can use your money to start their IRA up to the limit of their earnings. You get no tax deduction, of course.

Understanding Annuities: How Fixed and Variable Annuities Fit into Your Retirement Planning

I. A fixed annuity is like a long term, tax-sheltered CD.

   A. Advantages: It pays a fixed rate of return agreed upon up front and offers the tax-deferred compounding of your investment income. You know what to expect in terms of investment return.

   B. Disadvantages: You are "loaning" your money to an insurance company, and you could lose part or all of your investment if the company fails. There are also significant surrender charges if you cash your annuity in early.

   C. The financial rating services offer some guidance as to the relative safety of doing business with an insurance company, but they aren't foolproof. Limit yourself to insurers with only the highest ratings from two or more services.

II. A variable annuity is like a long term, tax-sheltered mutual fund.

A. Advantages: You control the investments. If you choose the right investment mix and a good performing product, variable annuities can be far more profitable than fixed annuities.

B. Disadvantages: You don't know what your annuity will eventually be worth; risk/reward is a two-edged sword. Also, the layers of fees make them more costly than simply buying mutual funds outright. And like fixed annuities, there are usually surrender charges if you decide to cash out early.

C. There are a few no-load variable annuities that have no surrender charges. They are relatively new with brief track records but are worth investigating.

In its simplest form, an annuity is a payment from an insurance company. You give the insurance company your money now...

...and they promise to give it back (plus a return on your investment) to you in the distant future (that's the deferred part). They credit your account as time goes along, but you don't actually get your money until much later. As long as the insurance company has your money, any gains credited to your account aren't taxable. When they finally start giving it back, any gains you receive are taxed at the tax rate you are paying in the year you get it back. This tax-deferment on your gains is the primary reason for considering an annuity.

The reason annuities get complicated is because of all the choices you have. The first and biggest decision you have to make is: Do you want to know in advance exactly how much your investment return will be (a fixed annuity) or are you willing to let the return vary depending on certain investment choices they let you make (a variable annuity)?

A fixed annuity is like a very long term, tax-sheltered CD.

It pays a fixed rate of return for an agreed upon period of time, just like a CD. The reason to buy a fixed annuity instead of just buying a CD is because you want the tax-shelter. But there are some drawbacks.

● Bank CDs are fully backed by the federal government up to $100,000, but fixed annuities are "guaranteed" only by the insurance company. The guarantee is only as strong as the financial strength of the company behind it. Many insurers have invested their own money in too many junk bonds (First Executive Life) and troubled real estate projects (Mutual Benefit). The collapse of five large insurers in 1991 jeopardized more than 500,000 annuity holders. If your insurer fails, you could be just like any other creditor trying to get his money back. And it doesn't matter where you buy your annuity; not even those sold by banks are federally insured.

● The "early withdrawal" penalty for cashing in a CD early is relatively mild (usually you forfeit a portion of the interest you've earned), but the "surrender charges" on annuities can be horrendous. The amount you receive if you cash in early is reduced by charges that start out as high as 7% of your capital the first year, typically dropping 1% per year until they disappear after the seventh year.

Some companies have no surrender charges, instead assessing "deferred sales charges," which you pay whether you take your money out or not. Thanks a lot. Others promise that you won't lose any of your principal if you cash in early—that means that the most you can lose is all the income you've earned. Still pretty steep. But all companies waive surrender charges in the event of your death; your beneficiary receives the total amount accumulated in your annuity.

● If you take your money out of an annuity before age 59½, the IRS hits you with a 10% penalty tax on your earnings. This is in addition to the normal income tax. Remember: Just because the insurer is willing to forgo surrender charges *doesn't mean* you won't have to pay the IRS's penalty tax for cashing in early.

● Here are some points to consider when comparing rates offered by various fixed annuities: (1) The fixed rate promised is only good for so many years; after that the insurer can lower the rate at its discretion; (2) So-called "bonus" and "tiered-rate" annuities, which promise high returns during the first year, usually pay either lower rates down the road or they impose unpleasant restrictions on when and how you can get your money back; and (3) Tax "deferred" is not the same as tax "free." Don't fall for promotions which imply that a 7% return on an annuity is like an 11% pre-tax return on a CD. You do *eventually* have to pay taxes on your annuity earnings; they're not tax free.

Don't forget to consider the credit risk. Fixed annuities are just another way for insurers to borrow money.

Fixed annuities, guaranteed investment contracts, and cash value life insurance policies are all products where it's possible for you to lose part or all of your money. The publicity that surrounded the problems of several insurers in 1991 made clear to investors the importance of dealing with a financially strong insurance company.

At this point, it's too early to say how widespread the problem of insolvent insurers will become. Insurance industry spokesmen are quick to say that the industry is sound overall and that it was the economic downturn of 1990-1991 coupled with poor management at some companies that led to the recent failures. However, there are voices within the industry itself that are also raising these questions. For example, IDS Life Insurance issued a report suggesting as much as 20% of the industry could be in trouble if there were to be a very severe recession.

Given that insurance companies have the image of being stodgy, conservative, and safe, it's difficult for many to understand how they got into this mess. Here's how it happened.

The high interest rates in the early 1980s made the low returns offered by life insurance policies unattractive to individuals. Rather than looking at their life insurance as "protection," they increasingly regarded it as an "investment." The industry was forced to redesign its products in order to stay competitive. Companies came out with new kinds of cash value policies and annuities that promised better returns. The "guaranteed investment contract" (GIC) was invented so the industry would have a more appealing product to offer employer-sponsored retirement plans. These products were successful, but their very success had a dramatic impact on the industry's mix of policies. Whereas in 1969, only 26% of the policies written were annuities and pensions, 20 years later this number had grown to 67%.

The problem with this is the pressure it put on the insurers to earn higher returns on their own investment portfolios in order to pay the higher rates they were promising investors. This ultimately led them into higher risk areas, most notably the "junk" bond market and the commercial real estate market. Both of these areas are high risk, but they differ in the seriousness of the consequences if problems arise.

Money lost in the junk bond market through defaults is usually gone forever. A survey of insurance companies shows an average of 24% of their portfolio in junk bonds; critics suggest a 5%-10% ceiling is in order. One reason the Executive Life failure was so costly is that the company had about two-thirds of its assets in junk, a dangerous level by almost any standard.

A soft economy increases office vacancies and decreases retail spending. This pushed some of the marginal commercial developments over the edge. Still, real estate loans in foreclosure, given sufficient time to find a buyer, usually have a reasonable expectancy of recouping some or most of the money at risk. Mutual Benefit Life's troubles were due to its real estate portfolio. Whereas the industry average is about 22% of invested assets, Mutual Benefit had committed 40%

to real estate loans. This need not have become a problem, but Mutual Benefit took other steps that greatly increased its risk. Not only did it concentrate its loans in relatively fewer developments than prudent diversification would require, the company also invested in some of the bigger projects as well as loaned money to them. So if a project got into trouble, there was a conflict between Mutual Benefits' interests as a lender versus its interests as an owner. The owner side won, leading the company to continue loaning funds to the problem developments in order to keep them going. By the time regulators took charge of Mutual Benefit, about 10% of its $5 billion real estate and mortgage-loan portfolio was in trouble.

Unfortunately, you can't rely on state regulators to completely protect you. They are often overworked and understaffed.

That's why they keep working with problem companies. Most state funds are not capable of handling large-scale problems, so the hope is that by keeping these insurers operating, the problems will be corrected given time. Delay is the accepted strategy.

When regulators come in to reorganize or sell an insurer, their first responsibility is to protect the present policyholders as much as possible. In order to do this, they usually "freeze" the company assets in order to keep control of as much of the money as possible while they sort out the

State Insurance
Departments

Your state department of
insurance can be a helpful
source of information
on the companies doing
busines in your state.
Don't be bashful about calling.

Alabama 205-269-3550
Alaska 907-562-3626
Arizona 602-255-5400
Arkansas 501-371-1325
California 800-927-4357
Colorado 303-866-6400
Connecticut 203-297-3800
Delaware 800-282-8611
Florida 800-342-2762
Georgia 404-656-2056
Hawaii 800-468-4644
Idaho 208-334-2250
Illinois 217-782-4515
Indiana 800-622-4461
Iowa 515-281-5705
Kansas 800-432-2484
Kentucky 502-564-3630
Louisiana 504-342-5301
Maine 207-582-8707
Maryland 800-492-7521
Massachusetts 617-727-7189
Michigan 517-373-0240

damage. This means that, for the time being, policyholders are no longer allowed to cash in their life insurance policies or annuities, move them to another insurer, or even borrow against them. The most important activities, like paying death benefits and mailing out the payments on annuities and GICs, usually continue in the normal fashion.

Will policyholders in investment-type products eventually receive 100% of what they're entitled to after the regulators sort things out? Maybe. It depends on if there's enough money left to go around. If not, the regulators make enough reductions in the benefit payments so that the policyholders share proportionately in what funds are available. That's apparently what will happen in the California Executive Life case, where regulators are proposing that cash policy and annuity values be reduced to reflect the value of the remaining assets on hand. (They've already reduced the monthly annuity payments by 30%). The fate of investors who hold their GICs is uncertain.

Only limited protection is offered by the various insurance rating organizations.

In fact, the highly publicized A.M. Best ratings are looking increasingly meaningless. For example, Executive Life carried an A+ from Best until it disclosed massive junk bond losses in early 1990. Even then, it was only downgraded to an A. And Mutual Benefit enjoyed an A+ from Best until just 10 days before state regulators moved in.

There are now five major ratings services: A.M. Best, Duff & Phelps, Moody's, Standard & Poor's, and Weiss Research. Best is the oldest and rates the largest number of firms (around 1,400) but is *known for its leniency and releases its ratings only with the insurance company's permission.* The next three ratings firms charge insurers $15,000 to $25,000 a year to include them in their ratings, which explains why there is a much smaller number of insurance firms in their data bases (Duff & Phelps rates 61 companies, Moody's 72, and S&P 450). Weiss is the newest rating service on the scene, and it has quickly

Minnesota 800-652-9747
Mississippi 800-562-2957
Missouri 800-726-7390
Montana 406-444-2040
Nebraska 402-471-2201
Nevada 800-992-0900
New Hampshire 800-852-3416
New Jersey 609-292-5360
New Mexico 505-827-4500
New York 800-342-3736
North Carolina 800-662-7777
North Dakota 800-247-0560
Ohio 800-686-1526
Oklahoma 800-522-0071
Oregon 503-378-4271
Pennsylvania 717-787-5173
Rhode Island 401-277-2223
South Carolina 800-768-3467
South Dakota 605-773-3563
Tennessee 800-342-4029
Texas 800-252-3439
Utah 801-538-3800
Vermont 802-828-3301
Virginia 800-552-7945
Washington 800-562-6900
Washington, D.C. 202-727-8000
West Virginia 800-642-9004
Wisconsin 800-236-8517
Wyoming 307-777-7401

become the most controversial because of its tougher, strictly by-the-numbers approach. Only 6% of the 1700+ life insurers covered in its current directory get the B+ or higher grades necessary to land on Weiss's recommended list.

To find out if your insurer is in good health...

...put your agent to work. You paid him a sizable commission not only to sell you the annuity policy but also to service it. Tell him you want to know the ratings on your insurer from Weiss and any of the others that publish a rating for it.

If your agent fails to satisfy your concerns, here are two other options. Standard and Poor's (212-208-8000 / Ratings Information Line) offers a free service where they will tell you over the phone the current ratings on the 450 insurers they cover. There is a limit of five ratings per call. Alternately, Weiss Research (800-289-9222) will send you a one-page "safety brief" on your insurer, which contains their latest rating and an easy-to-understand update of the major factors behind it. There is a $25 charge for this service. Remember, due to the different ratings systems devised by these two firms, you cannot compare them to one another—a C+ rating from Weiss might be comparable to an AA rating from S&P. Be sure you get a copy of the definitions describing what the ratings mean.

If you're considering moving your annuity to another insurer, here are some costs to keep in mind. First, there are surrender penalties that routinely cost 7% during the first year of a policy, dropping 1% per year until they finally stop. Second, there are also tax consequences if you cash out of a policy (without doing a "1035 exchange") and receive more back than you paid in premiums. If you do decide that a move is best, be sure to do a 1035 exchange. Your agent can provide the form you need. This will continue the tax-deferral on the earnings in your cash-value policies and annuities.

Although the reports of several insurance failures in succession is unsettling, it can lead to a positive long-term result. As Americans shift to the stronger firms, the result will be a healthier insurance industry and economy. At the same time, those insurers who have remained strong by taking their fiduciary responsibilities seriously and following a prudent investment course will be rewarded.

Now, let's switch our focus to "variable" annuities.

They circumvent the insurance company credit risk by giving you control of the investments. Think of them as mutual funds wrapped up in a tax-sheltered package. Unlike a fixed annuity, where you are essentially loaning money to the insurance company and, in return, agree upon a rate of return up front, the returns in a variable annuity aren't locked in ahead of time. They vary depending on how well the investments perform—that's why they're called "variable."

The variable annuity has one major advantage over the fixed kind—you have control over the investments. Most insurance companies include at least three investment choices in their variable annuities: a blue chip stock fund, a bond fund, and a money market fund. They let you decide how much of the money you give them goes into each category. Your eventual return is affected by three things.

❶ **Your allocation decisions.** If you decide to put all your money into the stock market fund just before a major sell-off, you'll get off to a slow start. On the other hand, if you play it safe in the money market fund, you're giving up the reason for choosing the variable kind in the first place—greater profit potential.

❷ **Investment fund performance.** It could be that even though you make excellent allocation decisions, the funds offered by your particular insurer just don't perform well. Just like mutual funds, some finish in the top ranks year after year while others are perennial also-rans. Check out the track records of the funds in the variable annuity being offered to you. How do they compare with other variable annuity funds over the same period?

❸ **Fees, fees, and fees.** There are three kinds of fees you have to pay with most variable annuity products. First, there are the sales fees, usually disguised as "surrender charges." Most annuities don't have an up-front sales charge; instead the cost of commissions paid to the brokers and insurance agents is partially recovered by penalties paid if investors take their money out of the annuity in the first seven years.

Next come the "contract fees," which include annual administrative and insurance fees. Among their other purposes, these fees guarantee that your beneficiaries won't get back less than you put in, regardless of how poorly your investment choices perform. According to Lipper Analytical Services, these fees average about 1.3% per year. You pay these every year you own the annuity.

Finally there are the fees paid to the investment managers who make the portfolio decisions in the funds. These are similar to the management fees paid by shareholders of regular mutual funds and typically run about 1% per year. These also are ongoing.

So you can see how the overhead expenses cut into your returns by about 2.3% each and every year, even assuming you hold your annuity longer than seven years and avoid the surrender charges. Another drawback is the loss of liquidity. Annuities are designed for retirement planning and are intended as long-term investments. Once you put your money into one, you're supposed to leave it there until at least age 59½. If you take it out sooner, you get hit with a 10% penalty from the government, just as with IRAs.

Are variable annuities worth the cost and red tape?

The payoff for putting up with these limitations and drawbacks is the long term, tax-deferred compounding of your profits. A variable annuity is a good fit for you if:

- You've already made the full $2,000 contribution to your IRA.

- You've paid the maximum into an employer-sponsored 401(k) plan.

- You've got investment money you're willing to lock away for at least 10 years, which is the time needed to make up for the fees.

- You won't need your money before age 59½.

- You're in the 28% or 33% tax bracket where the tax-deferral aspects are most valuable.

If you think a variable annuity makes sense for you, great. That means it's time to look at specific alternatives.

The first decision to make is whether to contact your favorite insurance agent or stockbroker...

...or to go the do-it-yourself route. I heartily recommend the latter, mainly because you'll save a lot on either front-end commissions or the redemption charges (exit fees) on withdrawals, which come later. While there is a move in the direction of truly no-load variable annuities, at present I am aware of only three that are available for purchase. They are offered by Charter/Scudder, Mutual of America, and Vanguard, and are completely free of all sales charges, including surrender charges.

Variable annuities come with a variety of frills, some helpful, others merely confusing the issue. When you're shopping, three questions worth asking are:

❶ "How many subaccount choices do you offer and what are they?" (In annuity lingo, "subaccount" is another name for what you ordinarily call a mutual fund.) This question lets you know what kind of variety you will have to select from as you make the investment decisions in your annuity.

❷ "Do you allow telephone switching? If so, how often? Is there a charge?" Telephone switching allows you to transfer your money between the various investments offered with a simple phone call.

❸ "Do you offer a dollar-cost-averaging option?" This enables you to set up a schedule for automatically moving your money into stock and bond funds at regular intervals over time (in order to reduce the risk of moving at the wrong time).

On page 47, you'll find some performance information for three of the most popular types of subaccount categories. I've included the no-loads as well as some of the leading competition. The "rank" shows how each subaccount stacks up against competing funds with the same investment objectives. It is the total return from your annuity that will ultimately determine your degree of satisfaction.

Let's now return for a final look at the Millers' situation. You'll recall they still had a shortfall...

...in their projected retirement capital of $348,821. If we fast-forward 12 years to the time when they complete paying off their home mortgage, we find they have an extra $843 monthly surplus that had previously gone toward their monthly payment. Assuming they could average a 9% return in a variable annuity product over the remaining 18 years before retirement, how much of that monthly $843 should go into a variable annuity? By returning to the monthly compounding table in the IRA secition, we see that a 9% return will generate $13,509 over 18 years *for every "unit" of $25 per month invested*. From this we can compute that the Millers need to invest about $645 each month in order to reach their goal ($348,821 needed, divided by $13,509 for each $25 unit = 25.8 units, times $25 = $645 per month).

As we have seen, the process of planning for retirement requires you to do a lot of guessing about financial matters extending decades into the future—what inflation will be like, how much monthly budget surplus you will have, and what rates of return your investments will earn. Also, we're assuming the government will keep the current tax laws and Social Security programs pretty much as they are (and we *know* that's not likely).

So you must accept that it's impossible to make your projections with pinpoint accuracy and be ready to "run the numbers" again as new data become available. Now that you've been given the explanations, compound interest tables, and the example of the Millers presented in this section, you have the base of knowledge needed to stay on top of this very important area. ♦

TOTAL RETURNS FROM SELECTED VARIABLE ANNUITIES

FOR 12 MONTHS ENDING 30 JUNE 1992

Sponsor	Growth Stocks		Corp Bonds		Stock/Bond Mix	
	Return	Rank	Return	Rank	Return	Rank
Charter/Scudder	17.6%	1	14.0%	4	16.2%	2
Mutual of America	17.3%	2	13.7%	4	8.8%	10
Vanguard	12.3%	5	12.1%	8	12.2%	6
AmerCapital/Nationwide	14.1%	5	17.3%	1	12.6%	6
Anchor National ICAP II	11.9%	6	12.0%	9	10.5%	9
Fidelity Retiremnt Reserve	16.9%	2	12.4%	7	13.5%	4
Hartford Life / Director	6.8%	10	13.1%	5	8.7%	10
Lincoln National Multi-Fund	8.9%	9	13.8%	4	10.8%	8
Mass Mutual Flex V	13.0%	4	12.8%	6	13.4%	4
MONY Master	15.6%	3	14.1%	3	20.5%	1
Northwestern Mutual	7.7%	9	13.1%	5	9.9%	9
Prudential Discovery Plus	10.1%	8	13.1%	5	9.8%	9
Travelers Universal Annuity	10.0%	8	10.9%	10	11.3%	7
Industry Average	**12.7%**		**12.9%**		**12.9%**	

Notes: I only have room to show a sampling of variable annuity products; there are hundreds on the market. Most variable annuities have four to six investment choices (called "subaccounts") to choose from; I have shown only the three basic ones. For each listing, I show the total return for the twelve months ending 6/30/92. Next to the return, on a scale from 1 to 10, I show how that portfolio ranked in comparison to its competitors in the same risk category. 1 means a finish in the top 10% of its peer group, while a 10 indicates a bottom 10% finish. Performance is constantly changing, so a performance evaluation should not be made solely on the basis of this small sample. Most variable annuities have surrender charges that decline on a sliding scale over time. Charter National / Scudder (800-225-2470), Mutual of America (212-399-1600), and Vanguard (800-522-5555) are the only true no-loads at present.

The Outrageous Truth About Social Security

I. The truth about Social Security is that it is a wealth transfer program, much like welfare. It takes money from one group of citizens (active workers) and gives it to another group of citizens (inactive workers).

A. It is not an "insurance" program because the amount you put in has no correlation to the amount you receive back. It does not "entitle" you to benefits because Congress can legally reduce them any time it chooses.

B. There is no "trust fund" set aside to be invested for future retirees, and so there can be no "surplus." Part of the payroll taxes coming in are transferred directly to retirees, the rest are "borrowed" and spent immediately on federal programs.

C. Workers do not make "contributions" that "earn" them protection. Workers pay taxes that earn them nothing.

II. When the baby-boomer generation enters retirement, there will be an inadequate number of active workers to tax. To balance the books:

A. Changes will be needed that require active workers to pay more in taxes each year as well as work for more years before retiring.

B. Changes will be needed that decrease the level of monthly income that retired workers can expect to receive.

When George Orwell wrote his classic novel *1984*, he coined the expression "doublethink."

The ruling government ("Big Brother") used doublethink language to make lies sound truthful and to give an appearance of virtue where there was none. Our own government has proven masterful at this in the words it has used to promote the Social Security program.

From the very founding of our country, most Americans believed that caring for the elderly was a private matter between family members. While Christian charities, churches, and state and local governments would often assist those with special needs, the basic responsibility remained with the individual. This all changed with the passing of the Social Security Act of 1935. For the first time, it became morally acceptable for the government to confiscate money from one group of citizens for the sole purpose of just giving it away to another group of citizens. *Responsibility for the elderly was being transferred from the individual/family to society.* In order to overturn our 150-year tradition of self-reliance, doublethink wording was used to make this transition more acceptable to the American people.

Doublethink Example #1:
We're told we're buying "insurance."

To disguise the fact that Social Security is actually a wealth-transfer program, the government named it "Old Age and

Survivors Insurance." After all, buying insurance is a prudent financial step every family should take, isn't it? But insurance involves making payments proportionate to the risk involved. That's why insurance companies hire actuaries—to help them set premiums based on reasonable life expectancies. Social Security isn't like insurance at all; your payments have little direct correlation to your ultimate benefits.

This immediately became obvious with the case of Ida Fuller. Before retiring in 1939, she had paid a mere $22 into Social Security. In her first month, she recouped all that she had ever paid in! By the time she left this life 34 years later at the age of 100, she had collected more than $20,000—almost 1,000 times more than she had put in!

In *Beyond Our Means*, Alfred Malabre describes a different, but equally compelling, scenario:

> Consider a worker who began paying into the system in 1937, when it was launched, and worked until 1982. If he had paid the *maximum* in Social Security taxes each of the 45 working years, his payments would have totaled $12,828. His benefits would have begun at $734 a month. If he were married, his wife would collect half of his benefit, or an additional $367 monthly, bringing their total first-year benefit to $13,217, or more than he had paid in the forty-five years of employment.

Malabre goes on to show that if the couple live out normal life expectancies, their lifetime benefits would amount to some $375,000! You may wonder how all this lavish generosity is possible. We'll take that up shortly.

Doublethink Example #2:
We're told we're "entitled" to benefits.

We're led to believe that, upon retirement, our years of payments give us specific entitlement rights. That is, the government is obligated to honor its commitments. Unfortunately, that's not the case. The fact is that the government can change the rules anytime it wants. For example, it used to be that you could retire at age 65 with "full benefits." In 1983, as part of a Social Security bailout plan, Congress decided to raise the age requirements on a graduated basis. Now, people (like me) who were born between 1943-1954 have to work until age 66 to get full benefits. That involves not merely waiting an additional year to collect, but also an additional year of paying in. So, what I had been promised for half of my working life is suddenly changed at the stroke of a pen. Congress giveth and Congress taketh away.

Is that fair? No less an authority that the U.S. Supreme Court has ruled that Congress can do whatever it wants with Social Security, saying,

> The Social Security program *is in no sense a federally-administered insurance program* under which each worker pays premiums over the years and acquires at retirement an indefeasible [guaranteed] right to receive for life a fixed monthly benefit irrespective of the conditions which Congress has chosen to impose from time to time [emphasis added].

Doublethink Example #3:
We're told our money goes into a "trust fund."

For most of us, the expression "trust fund" means that a sum of money is being accumulated, invested safely, and is growing daily as it awaits the time when it will be needed. It sounds secure. Unfortunately, nothing could be further from the truth. The Social Security program has not set aside any trust money for our future use, and it never has. Actually the program is more like the world's largest chain letter.

Remember the examples I gave you earlier about the people receiving huge sums in relation to what they put in? Since their withholdings couldn't have grown that much purely from investments, how was it possible? Here's how they did it. From the millions of dollars of "contributions" coming into Social Security each morning from the younger workers, they took what they needed in order to pay the generous "benefits" in the afternoon to the older retired workers. What did they do with the rest? They "invested" it in Treasury bonds. In other words, Social Security loaned what was left to the federal government to spend on whatever it wanted. That money is long gone; only the IOUs remain.

The federal government is very good at borrowing; it is very bad when it comes to paying back. It is so bad, in fact, that America has now become the world's largest debtor nation. Where will the government come up with the money when Social Security comes knocking at its door with trillions of dollars of government IOUs in hand?

Doublethink Example #4:
We're told we're making "contributions" that "earn" us protection.

Money is automatically taken out of our paychecks and called a "contribution." But unlike voluntary payments into a private pension plan, there's nothing voluntary about these so-called contributions. Try to get the government to stop the withholding and see what happens. The simple fact is that Social Security is a tax.

A majority of working Americans *now pay more in Social Security withholdings than they do in federal income taxes.* What started out as a 1% payroll tax with a $30 per year maximum per person is now a 7.65% tax with an annual maximum of $4,085. For the average worker, that means it takes almost one month's wages each year just to pay his Social Security taxes!

Now, I might not consider this to be all that bad if I thought my own turn would come—if, like Malabre's worker, I would get back all that I had paid in during my very first year of retirement, and that I would eventually reap lifetime benefits that were almost 30 times more than the total taxes I paid. But, alas, I harbor no such illusions; I know the awful truth about the so-called surplus.

Doublethink Example #5:
We're told that Social Security is running a "surplus."

As appalling as all of the foregoing has been, it now gets even worse. You will hear that Social Security is running a surplus that was projected to exceed $225 billion by the end of 1991 and to reach $9.3 *trillion* by the year 2030. This is supposed to be reassuringly good news. Here are two reasons why it's not.

First, they can't know if the projections are correct in saying there will be $9.3 trillion in surplus in 2030. The Social Security trustees are making some very optimistic assumptions about inflation staying low, unemployment staying low, the birthrate rising, and life expectancies *not* rising. If things don't go as planned (and when do they?), there will be a huge shortfall. Yet, it will be impossible to raise Social Security taxes high enough to bridge the gap. A former chief actuary for the Social Security Administration estimated that individual payroll taxes would have to be raised from their present 7.65% rate to *more than 20.0%* just to pay all the benefits currently being promised. Is it realistic to think that the next generation will tolerate increases of that magnitude? Should they? Not a chance. All in all, it wouldn't be surprising if, 40 years out, the projections are off a mere trillion dollars or so.

Second, in the unlikely event that the surplus projection for 2030 is right on target, Social Security will still need to start cashing in those trillions of dollars in Treasury IOUs in order to come up with the hard cash needed to pay out the monthly benefits. And, as we've already seen, there's no money set aside for this. In the great doublethink tradition, what Congress likes to call a $9.3 trillion surplus is actually a gigantic $9.3 trillion future liability!

Sounds pretty hopeless, doesn't it? Just how hopeless depends on...

...how close *you personally* are to the day you switch teams— leaving the ranks of the people paying in and joining those in that happy state of grace where you receive monthly income for life far in excess of your earlier contributions.

If you are planning to retire in the next 10 years, you're in pretty good shape. There may be minor adjustments to your benefits along the way, but congressional hypocrisy and cowardice is probably good for another decade of failure to face up to Social Security's monumental problems.

The rest of us are probably going to be pretty unhappy about whatever "fix" Congress finally comes up with, and the younger we are now, the more unhappy we're likely to be. In the past, each generation of workers was asked to support the benefits for the previous generation. But it is falling to the baby-boomer generation to pay for the retirement of not only the previous generation (the workers who supported Ida Fuller so generously) but also to provide trillions in additional taxes for their own retirement as well.

Today's workers carry the triple burden of (1) paying far more in Social Security taxes than any previous generation, (2) waiting longer to collect than any previous generation, and (3) retiring with lower after-tax benefits than any previous generation. As unfair as this is, tomorrow's workers, our children, might have to pay even more, wait even longer, and receive even less. And that's why the truth about Social Security is indeed outrageous.

In light of the uncertainties surrounding the level of Social Security benefits after 2010, receiving significant support from the private pension plans sponsored by your employer is all the more critical. A basic understanding of their strengths and weaknesses is essential if you are to plan realistically. ◆

HOW MUCH WILL YOU RECEIVE FROM SOCIAL SECURITY?

Estimated Annual Benefit for Single Retiree at Normal Retirement Age* with Average and Maximum Covered Earnings

Year	Average	Maximum
1995	$10,734	$14,966
2000	13,669	19,802
2005	18,333	27,529
2010	22,483	34,792
2015	28,833	45,532
2020	39,786	63,034
2025	48,506	76,909
2030	60,594	96,073
2035	77,700	123,192
2040	99,644	157,866

Beneficiaries are assumed to have been full-time workers earning the average wage in covered employment, or the maximum covered wage throughout their working lives. Married couples with a spousal benefit would receive 150% of the amounts shown in the table. *Normal retirement age gradually moves from 65 to 67 after the turn of the century. 1991 Annual Report of the Board of Trustees of the Federal Old-Age and Survivors Insurance Trust Fund.

Your Pension at Work: Understanding Defined-Benefit Plans

I. **Employer-sponsored pension plans that promise to pay a specific dollar amount when you retire are called "defined-benefit" plans.**

   A. There are usually eligibility requirements to be met in terms of the length of time you've been with the company before you can participate in the plan.

   B. The amount of your retirement benefit is computed according to a formula which takes many variables into account. Among them are your: salary and age at retirement, years with the company, Social Security benefits, and the survivors' benefit you select.

II. **You should understand fully the circumstances under which you will receive a retirement benefit and how the benefit will be computed.**

A. You are entitled to receive annual financial reports from your company, which contain information about the plan as well as your personal benefit.

B. If your company goes bankrupt before you retire, there is a chance your benefit will be affected. The Pension Benefit Guaranty Corporation exists to insure your benefit, but, much as the FSLIC proved to be during the S&L crisis, it is considerably underfunded.

C. Your best defense is to maintain an active, informed interest in all affairs affecting your company plan.

Although the government itself can change its rules anytime it wants and arbitrarily reduce...

...the Social Security benefits you've been "contributing" to for a working lifetime, it won't let *your employer* do that to you. After all, that wouldn't be fair. (Congress loves to apply one set of standards to itself and a completely different set to the rest of us!) So let's look at employer-sponsored pension plans to see what help you can expect from your company. First, you should understand that there are two different kinds of pension plans. One kind promises only to put a certain amount aside for you each year but makes no projections as to the amount of your ultimate monthly benefit. This kind is called a "defined-contribution" plan, and comes in a bewildering array of alphabet-like names such as SEP-IRA, MPP, and TSAs like the 401(k) and 403(b). I'll deal with these plans in the next section.

For now, let's concentrate on the other type of pension plan, the kind that has been the overwhelming preference of business, industry, and state and local governments. Of all American workers who were covered by an employer-sponsored pension plan in 1990, about 70% of them had this plan as their primary pension coverage.

These "defined-benefit" plans promise to pay you, when you retire, a certain dollar amount every month for as long as you live...

...however, they promise nothing about how much money your company will put aside each year to accomplish this (other than observe certain minimum federal requirements). These plans are called "defined-benefit" plans because the focus is on the *lifetime monthly benefit* you'll ultimately receive. Under this arrangement, the employer carries the burden of where the money for the contributions comes from as well as how well the investments do between now and your retirement.

The first barrier standing between you and your monthly pension check is meeting the eligibility requirements. Just because you've been hired doesn't mean you immediately qualify for their retirement plan. Usually they require (1) that you've reached a certain age, and (2) have been with the company for a certain period of time before you qualify to join the plan. It is customary that an employee must be at least 21 years old and have been with the company at least one year.

Once you're eligible, what you really want to know is...

...how much is my monthly benefit going to be when I retire? That depends on several factors. Each is fairly simple; let's take them one at a time.

● **Salary formula.** The goal of a monthly pension check is to help replace the earnings lost when you retire. That means your benefit is based primarily on the amount of your annual earnings while you were still working. Some formulas take an average of your earnings from all the years you worked for the company. Presumably, the earlier years were not as well paying, so this is not as favorable to you as a plan that uses a formula based on your final year(s) of service.

● **Years of service.** People who spent their entire career with the same company receive more than those who come along later. That's why your benefit is affected by the number of years you work for your employer. But how many hours are needed to constitute a "year of service?" Some plans may require 500 hours in a 12-consecutive month period while others require 1000 hours. Or what if you worked for 20 years, left for 2 years, and returned for another 18 years? Do you get credit for 38 years or just the last 18 years? There are countless variations on this theme that can affect your benefit.

● **Vesting requirements.** When can you know for sure that you're guaranteed to receive at least some pension benefit from your employer? The year you qualify to join the plan? After three years with the company? That's where the concept of "vesting" comes in. It means you have an absolute right to receive some money from a retirement plan, even if you resign or are fired. You're entitled to it no matter what. The most favorable is "vesting upon entry" where you must wait for two years before qualifying to participate in the plan, but are immediately 100% vested upon entry. This is especially helpful to working women who, on average, change jobs more frequently than men.

● **Normal retirement age.** Most plans use formulas that consider 65 as the normal retirement age. If you choose to work past 65 (federal law prohibits age discrimination rules that would *require* you to retire before age 70), will your plan give you credit for the additional years worked? Or what if you wanted to take early retirement, how much will that reduce your monthly pension check? The rules governing these matters vary from plan to plan.

● **Social Security considerations.** So-called "integrated plans" deduct a portion of your monthly Social Security check from your monthly benefit check. Remember that your employer has already paid hefty Social Security taxes. From his point of view, it seems reasonable that the company retirement plan formula recognize that you are receiving Social Security benefits to which the company has already contributed.

● **Survivors' benefits.** As an alternative to the basic "monthly check for life" benefit, federal law requires most plans to offer you another approach: a joint and survivor annuity. If this is selected, the monthly benefit check doesn't stop coming when you die; it goes instead to your spouse (or whoever you may have named in the annuity). The trade-off is that your pension will be about 20% lower than it otherwise would be—after all, it has to last for two lifetimes now instead of just one—and the amount of the monthly check is cut in half when you pass on. Even so, it's good to know that your spouse will still be provided for.

Armed with this information, you might now be wondering how the plan at your company...

...measures up in these various areas. If you aren't sure, it's time to find out! Your employer is required by law to offer every participant a summary of the plan that's written in layman's terms. This is called a "summary plan description" and should be readily available from your personnel department. Ask for one. It will explain all of the above and lots more.

Many companies also provide a personalized "employee benefit statement" once a year that explains the amount of benefits you've earned to date and provides an estimate of how much your monthly retirement check will be. Other items that you're entitled to receive upon request include: the "summary annual report" (your plan's balance sheet), the Form 5500 (your plan's tax return and an excellent source of information concerning its financial health), and the retirement plan document itself (in case you happen to enjoy digging through page after page of mind-numbing legalese).

OK, let's stop and see where we stand. You now know how to find out what your company's pension benefit would be for a person with your years of service and salary history. You also know what you need to do to qualify for it.

Assuming you do your part, there's only one thing (and I hate to bring it up but somebody needs to tell you) that can go wrong—

—your company could reach retirement before you do, that is, your company goes into bankruptcy. To understand the possible consequences, it's time you were introduced to ERISA.

For the pension world, 1974 was a watershed year because of the passage of the Employee Retirement Income Security Act. For the first time, there were uniform federal guidelines, which all employer pension plans were required to follow. The major emphasis was on setting standards concerning which employees would be eligible for coverage, when they would receive vesting rights, and how employers should go about funding their plans to make sure the money was there to provide the benefits they promised. The new funding requirements revealed that many plans had inadequate reserves to meet the pension promises being made to their employees. These underfunded plans were required to build their reserves up to a fully funded position, but were given as long as 40 years to do so. That's why, almost 20 years after ERISA was passed, there are still companies that have underfunded plans. As long as these companies survive and are able to continue following their pension funding programs, retirees will receive all of the benefits to which they're entitled.

But what if a company goes under? Congress planned for that, too.

At the same time it passed ERISA, Congress created the Pension Benefit Guaranty Corporation (PBGC) to insure pension benefits in much the same way the FDIC insures bank deposits. This protection is funded by employers who must pay an annual premium for each participant. Of the 100,000 plans that the PBGC insures, more than half are generously overfunded (the 1980s bull market was a big help!). Even so, *there are some massive underfunded plans around, and they pose a major problem.* Consider this: When Pan American Airways filed for bankruptcy in late 1991, its biggest debt was an unfunded liability of $1 billion owed to its own defined-benefit plan! To date, the PBGC has taken over the responsibility for some 1,700 plans that were underfunded when the companies went into bankruptcy, including such well-known names as Eastern Airlines, Kaiser Steel, and Allis-Chalmers. Estimates of the PBGC's ultimate potential deficit range from $30-$40 billion! Welcome to the next financial crisis where the taxpayer foots the bill for irresponsible corporations.

OK, so that's the PBGC's problem (except it could become your problem too if taxes are raised to pay for all this.) I know you're more interested for now in making sure your pension is secure. What can you do? Here's what I suggest.

❶ **Ask your company if its defined-benefit plan is fully funded.** Unfortunately, even if you learn your plan is fully funded, you're still not home free (see item 2 below). You can also check with the PBGC, which periodically releases a list of the 50 U.S. companies with the most seriously underfunded plans. The current list includes familiar names such as Chrysler, Paine Webber, Rockwell, Honeywell, and Westinghouse.

❷ **Ask what assumptions your company is making about the kinds of investment returns it expects in the plan over the long term.** If a conservative number such as 7%-8% is being used, that's good because it's realistic. But if the company is counting on, as General Motors is, its plan investments to average 11% a year, it's on shaky ground. Unrealistically high assumptions make the plan's funding look better without improving the actual health of the plan.

❸ **If you have concerns about the adequacy of your plan's funding, contact the U.S. Department of Labor.** This agency serves as a watchdog of employee benefit programs and conducts inquiries into underfunded plans. The name and number of someone to contact should be listed in your plan's annual report.

❹ **Recognize the limitations of the insurance coverage.** If your plan falls into the hands of the PBGC, the current maximum benefit allowed is $27,000 a year. This could be less than your plan originally promised.

And one suggestion for retirees: If you've been provided with an annuity that your employer bought for you from an insurance company, keep close tabs on the financial health of the insurer. Many employers buy the annuities without regard to the financial strength of the insurer; low cost is often their primary criteria. ◆

Your Pension at Work: Making Sense of Defined-Contribution Plans

I. Employer-sponsored pension plans that follow formulas for paying specific dollar amounts into your retirement account each year are called "defined-contribution" plans.

A. These plans make no promises as to how much your benefit will be when you retire. Your retirement benefit will ultimately be determined by the amount and frequency of annual contributions and the investment performance experienced in your account.

B. Under such plans the risk of poor investment returns rests with the employee rather than the employer. That's why employees generally have significant control over the investment portfolios.

II. There is a variety of these plans with differing contribution requirements, limitations, and employer matching features. We discuss the key features of the major kinds of plans.

III. When you are ready to withdraw your benefits, these plans provide three alternative methods. Each has its own advantages, depending on your personal income and tax situation at that time.

    A. You can take your money in one large payment. The entire amount is taxed at ordinary rates in the year it is received, but you may qualify for income averaging, which spreads the tax liability over several years.

    B. You can have your account transferred to an IRA rollover and continue to enjoy tax-deferred growth.

    C. You can begin receiving monthly income payments for life.

The second major kind of employer-sponsored retirement plans are called "defined-contribution" plans because...

...they place their emphasis on how much the employer will put into the plan for you each year. No promises are made with respect to how much your account will be worth when you retire. In this respect, they are like IRAs. The advantage of this approach to employers should be readily apparent: *You* bear the investment risk between now and retirement rather than your company. If the investments do great, you'll have a healthy amount in the plan at retirement; if they perform poorly, you must make do with a lesser amount. This shift of the investment risk from the employer to you is significant; you no longer can "count on" having a specific monthly income.

But why look at the negatives? The flip side of this shift is that above-average investment performance in your account benefits you rather than your employer. Look at it as an opportunity! Here is another area that is now under your control where your Sound Mind strategy can help shape a balanced long-term portfolio that will be personalized to your specific goals and risk tolerance.

Over the years, Congress has created several varieties of defined-contribution plans. I've listed them in a table on the next page to give you an overview of the possibilities. Many companies have more than one of these plans in place in order to help you take the fullest advantage of the tax-sheltering possibilities. Though we cannot discuss all the complexities, the table will provide a general idea of the kinds of plans your employer offers. Then make an appointment with the appropriate person at your company to get your specific questions answered. I've also included some suggested questions to ask.

You should consider all of the investments over which you have decision-making authority, including those in your retirement accounts, as you analyze how best to diversify your portfolio to achieve the risk temperament you have elected to follow. By shifting some of your retirement plan holdings from stocks to bonds or vice versa, you can achieve the desired balance between equity and interest-earning investments.

Don't let the "guarantee" fool you. If you participate in a 401(k) retirement plan...

...chances are high that you have the option of allocating a portion of your account to a "guaranteed investment contract" (GIC). These are investment contracts sold by insurance companies to retirement plans that promise a specified rate of return over a one to five year period. They have been very popular because they usually offer yields up to 1% higher than those available from money funds or U.S. Treasury securities.

However, the money is not guaranteed at all. The contracts are backed only by the insurance companies that sell them. They're just IOUs. The word "guarantee" refers to the rate of return that's agreed upon at the outset, as in "rather than take

AN OVERVIEW OF THE MAJOR KINDS

Your company may offer one or more of the following defined-contribution pension plans. These are the most common types; however, there are many variations depending on the way your company's plan was initially structured.

TYPE OF PLAN	MONEY PURCHASE	PROFIT SHARING
Brief Summary	Your company agrees to contribute a certain percentage of your salary every year (even in unprofitable years). Can be either a corporate plan or, if employer is not incorporated, a Keogh plan.	Your company annually contributes a portion of its profits, if any, into a fund for employees. Can be either a corporate plan or, if employer is not incorporated, a Keogh plan.
What is the most you can put in each year?	You don't contribute.	You don't contribute.
What is the most your employer can put in each year?	25% of compensation or $30,000, whichever is less.	15% of compensation or $30,000 whichever is less.
Are annual contributions fixed at a certain amount?	Yes. The salary contribution formula must be followed each year.	No. The amount contributed can change from year to year.
When do you receive ownership rights to your pension?	Typically 3-7 years.	Typically 3-7 years.
Can you borrow from your account?	At the employer's discretion.	At the employer's discretion.

OF DEFINED-CONTRIBUTION PLANS

This is a highly technical area, and this table is merely intended to provide an overview. For more information on your specific rights and benefits, contact your company's human resources department.

SEP IRA	401(K) PLAN	403(B) PLAN
Simplified Employee Pensions use a form of employee IRAs rather than set up a separate company plan. Primarily funded by your employer, these accounts are highly portable if you change jobs.	A salary reduction plan where you decide how much of your salary to put in (up to a maximum level which is raised annually for inflation).The amount you contribute is not counted as taxable income.	Similar to the 401k plan, but limited to employees of public schools, government agencies, hospitals, religious organizations, and other nonprofit institutions.
Your normal $2,000 IRA contribution.	$8,994	$9,500
15% of compensation or $30,000, whichever is less.	Can match a percentage of your salary deferral up to 100%. Your contribution + employer's can't exceed $30,000 or 25% of your salary (after deducting your contribution), whichever is less.	Can match a percentage of your salary deferral up to 100%. Your contribution + employer's can't exceed $30,000 or 25% of your salary (after deducting your contribution), whichever is less.
No. The amount contributed can change from year to year.	No. The amount contributed can change from year to year.	No. The amount contributed can change from year to year.
Immediate.	Immediate on your contributions, but at the employer's discretion on any matching amounts.	Immediate on your contributions, but at the employer's discretion on any matching amounts.
No.	At the employer's discretion.	At the employer's discretion.

your chances in the stock market, we'll guarantee you 9% per year." That's all dandy as long as the insurance company prospers and is financially strong enough several years from now to honor its commitments. But because of bad investments in junk bonds and real estate, the creditworthiness of many insurance companies is now being questioned.

Employers are dealing with this concern in a variety of ways. Some are now buying GICs only from the highest rated insurance companies. Others are increasing the number of insurers with whom they do business in order to spread the risk around. Others have returned to Treasury securities, abandoning the GIC market completely. These changes are likely to mean that the fixed income portions in many 401(k) and other retirement plans will offer slightly lower returns. If this happens to you, don't complain about the lower rates; instead, thank your employer for protecting your retirement assets.

All of these plans have one thing in common: at some point, you're going to want to take your money out!

Your decision as to how to do this will be one of the most important and far-reaching ones of your financial life. You shouldn't make it hurriedly; in fact, you should begin thinking about it years ahead of time. Make sure you understand the laws (which Congress has succeeded in making complicated and confusing by changing them from time to time) and how they affect your range of options.

Some of the factors that will influence your decision include your age at retirement, birth year, health and life expectancy, income tax bracket, other sources of retirement income, inflationary expectations, desire for certainty versus desire for greater potential future income, and the list goes on.

Basically, you have three choices: to take all your money out in one large payment, to transfer your account value to an IRA rollover where you can continue to invest it on a tax-deferred basis, or to take it in the form of monthly payments spread over the remainder of your life. Here are some guidelines to consider as you go about making your decision. After finding out from your employer the amounts of both your lump-sum benefit and your monthly income benefit, ask yourself these questions:

● How long do I expect to live? Obviously, you can only make a guess based on your health at the time and your family history. The reason this comes into play is that the monthly payment option is usually computed based on a life expectancy of age 80. The longer you live past 80, the greater the value of your total monthly pension and the better off you are versus taking the lump sum.

● How dependent are my spouse or heirs on my estate? If your spouse is dependent on you, you might prefer the "joint and survivor" pension. It provides a monthly payment

THE THREE PRIMARY CHOICES FOR RECEIVING YOUR RETIREMENT BENEFITS

	Take Your Money in One Large Payment	Transfer Your Money to an IRA Rollover Account	Take Your Money in Monthly Payments
How do you receive your money?	Your employer pays your retirement benefit to you all at one time.	Your employer sends your entire retirement benefit directly to your new IRA account.	You choose the combination of amount and duration of guaranteed monthly payments.
What taxes will you pay?	The entire amount is taxed at ordinary income rates in the year it is received.	None until you begin making withdrawals (which will be taxed as income the year they are received).	The money you receive will be taxed as income the year it is received.
What other factors come into play?	A special tax formula may apply depending on your age or birth year. Early withdrawal penalty could apply if you are under age 59½. You lose your ability to continue investing on a tax-deferred basis.	Your investments continue to grow tax-deferred and are under your direct supervision. Early withdrawal penalty could apply if you are under age 59½ and begin making withdrawals immediately.	Early withdrawal penalty could apply if you are under age 59½ and do not choose the lifetime income option. If your employer provides your monthly payments by buying an annuity for you, a financially strong insurance company is of great importance.

to you for life (about 20% lower than it would otherwise be), with an ongoing monthly payment (reduced by half) to your spouse after your death. If providing for your spouse is a primary consideration, these and other options should be explored fully with your pension administrator. If providing for heirs is important, then the lump-sum option is the way to go.

● How do I feel about inflation? Unless your monthly benefit provides for adequate cost-of-living increases, you may find it difficult keeping up with inflation over the longer term. The lump-sum approach gives you the responsibility and risk of investing. For planning purposes, you might conservatively assume that you can obtain an average annual pre-tax return of 8%.

● What other sources of income will I have? Both options have their risks: the lump-sum the risk of doing your own investing, and the monthly payment the risk of keeping ahead of inflation. You should also consider what additional help you can expect from Social Security and your investments.

The table on the preceeding page summarizes the tax implications and other important features of each of the three alternatives. For additional help, I encourage you to contact some of the leading no-load organizations. Just tell them you are facing this very important decision of whether to take your retirement in a lump sum or roll it into an IRA. They've developed some user-friendly explanatory material (Schwab,

Fidelity, Dreyfus, and Price have done an especially good job), which will walk you through the technical aspects. All of these organizations offer their help free of charge because they're hoping to win you over as a long-term customer during your retirement years.

Be careful when "rolling out" of your company's pension plan—the rules changed in 1993!

Formerly you were given 60 days to deposit your lump sum benefit check into an IRA rollover in order to avoid any tax bite and preserve your tax-deferred program. Beginning January 1, 1993, your benefit check will be hit with a 20% withholding rate if it's made out to you. You can avoid the withholding by removing yourself from the transfer process. Arrange in advance for your employer to send your money directly to your new IRA roll-over account. This is called a trustee-to-trustee transfer.

I.R.S.

Why change the old way, which was working fine? Under the guise of wanting to encourage workers not to elect the lump sum option (where they might spend it rather than save it), the new law seems to be primarily motivated by a need to help finance additional jobless benefits for the unemployed. The government says it expects to gather in $2.1 billion from those unsuspecting citizens who are unaware that the rules have been changed. Again. ◆

Sound Mind Investing

THE FINANCIAL JOURNAL FOR TODAY'S CHRISTIAN FAMILY

Dear Valued Reader:

I hope this booklet has been helpful to you. If so, I believe you'd enjoy reading through a complimentary issue of my monthly *Sound Mind Investing* financial newsletter. It's based on biblically-based values and priorities (see pages 4-5), and gives you:

Help in setting and achieving realistic, personalized goals. You'll find no claims that I can predict coming economic events or market turns. Mine is a slow-but-sure, conservative strategy that emphasizes controlling your risk according to your age, goals, and personal investing temperament.

Very specific, timely advice. I recommend specific no-load mutual funds. For each of four different risk categories, I not only tell you what *what to buy* and *how much to buy*, but just as importantly, *when to sell and buy something else*!

Monthly "economic earthquake" updates. I include an economic primer that will help you understand the implications of the unfolding economic tremors. Plus, there are data and graphs of various economic indicators that will be especially helpful in giving us fair warning if a crisis seems to be approaching.

I'd like you to have the opportunity to see these benefits for yourself. Send in the attached postage-paid card for your free issue—there's absolutely no obligation to subscribe. I hope to hear from you soon!

Free!
A Sample Issue of
Sound Mind Investing

PLEASE DETACH BEFORE MAILING

☐ **Yes, send my free issue!**

Austin: I'm taking you up on your offer of a complimentary sample of your monthly *Sound Mind Investing* newsletter. Please send my free issue and subscription information to me at the address below.

Name: _____

Address: _____

City: _____

State: _____ Zip: _____

Free!
A Sample Issue of
Sound Mind Investing